Muffins
& cupcakes

by
Lawrence Rosenberg

The
AMERICAN
★ COOKING ★
GUILD™

Boynton Beach, Florida

Dedication
This book is dedicated to my mother and father for their love and encouragement, and for always being around to taste over the years; and to the memory of my grandfather, Sam Donowitz.

Acknowledgments
—Recipe Testing by Polly Clingerman and Joan Patten
—Cover Design and Layout by Pearl & Associates, Inc.
—Cover Photo by Burwell and Burwell
—Edited by Marian Levine
—Illustrations by Jim Haynes

Revised Edition 1997
Copyright © 1986 by Burwell & Burwell
All rights reserved.
Printed in U.S.A.
ISBN 0-942320-13-1

More...Quick Recipes for Creative Cooking!
The American Cooking Guild's *Collector's Series* includes over 30 popular cooking topics such as Barbeque, Breakfast & Brunches, Chicken, Cookies, Hors d' Oeuvres, Seafood, Tea, Coffee, Pasta, Pizza, Salads, Italian and many more. Each book contains more than 50 selected recipes. For a catalog of these and many other full sized cookbooks, send $1 to the address below and a coupon will be included for $1 off your first order.

Cookbooks Make Great Premiums!
The American Cooking Guild has been the premier publisher of private label and custom cookbooks since 1981. Retailers, manufacturers, and food companies have all chosen The American Cooking Guild to publish their premium and promotional cookbooks. For further information on our special markets programs please contact the address below.

The American Cooking Guild
3600-K South Congress Avenue
Boynton Beach, FL 33426

CONTENTS

Introduction

My specialty is cake decorating but one of my loves is baking. After all, what's the point of decorating a cake to look beautiful if the taste doesn't live up to expectations? In *Muffins & Cupcakes,* I'm sharing my favorite recipes with you.

Everyone loves muffins and cupcakes. Muffins can be eaten with your morning coffee, afternoon tea, or just for a snack during the day. My Stuffin' Muffin can be enjoyed as a main dish at any meal.

The cupcake recipes range from simple to elegant in appearance, yet all are relatively easy to make. I've also explained how to make and use a pastry bag for decorating your creations and I've provided an idea or two for decorating.

In sharing these ideas with other cooks, I offer my best wishes for happy baking.

Helpful Hints for Better Baking

- I like to preheat the oven 25° higher than the actual baking temperature called for in each recipe. This compensates for the heat loss that occurs when the oven door is opened. If you try this, don't forget to lower the heat by 25° as you slide the muffins into the oven.

- Use an oven thermometer to regulate the temperature of your oven. Oven gauges are often inaccurate and baking times will be thrown off.

- Fill any empty muffin wells with a little water to promote even baking.

- For better mixing, all refrigerated ingredients should be brought to room temperature.

- Use only solid shortening where called for, not butter or lard.

- If you like your cupcakes less sweet, use 1/4 cup less sugar or honey. It won't change the outcome but will suit your taste.

- For best results, use the freshest ingredients possible.

- Muffin batter should be mixed quickly, only until most of the dry ingredients are dampened. The batter will look lumpy. Over-mixed batter will make a tough muffin with tunnels.

Basic Muffins
& Variations

Basic Breakfast Muffins

These are great for breakfast! Serve them warm with butter and jam.

> 4 cups all-purpose flour
> 1/4 cup sugar
> 2 Tablespoons baking powder
> 1 teaspoon salt
> 2 cups milk
> 2 eggs
> 1/2 cup oil

Preheat oven to 400°. Grease muffin pans or prepare with liners.

In a large bowl, combine flour, sugar, baking powder and salt.

In a small bowl, combine milk, eggs and oil.

Fold wet ingredients into dry and mix just enough to moisten the dry ingredients.

Spoon batter into muffin pan, filling each well ⅔ full. Bake for approximately 20-25 minutes, or until a toothpick inserted in the center comes out clean and dry. Remove from oven and cool for ten minutes before turning muffins out of pans.

Yield: 24 muffins

Berry Muffins: You can use blueberries, blackberries, mulberries, raspberries or strawberries. To the basic batter, add ⅓ cup of sugar. Rinse and dry 1 cup of berries, sprinkle 2 tablespoons of flour over the berries and mix into the batter. Bake as above.

Cranberry Muffins: To the basic batter, add 1 cup of chopped or whole cranberries and ½ cup sugar. Bake as above.

Apple Raisin Muffins: To the basic muffin batter, mix in 1 teaspoon cinnamon, an extra ¼ cup sugar, 1 cup peeled, shredded apples and ½ cup dark raisins. Bake as above.

Date Nut Muffins: To the basic batter, mix in 1 cup of pitted dates (cut into small pieces) and 1 cup of chopped coarse walnuts.

Yellow Corn Muffins

These muffins are great served with fried chicken or other Southern style dishes.

1¹/3 cups all-purpose flour
3 teaspoons baking powder
1 teaspoon salt
2 Tablespoons sugar
³/4 cup yellow cornmeal
2 eggs, lightly beaten
1 cup milk
¹/4 cup unsalted butter, melted

Preheat oven to 425°.

Grease muffin pans or prepare with liners.

In a mixing bowl, whisk together the flour, baking powder, salt, sugar and cornmeal.

Add eggs, milk and butter to bowl. Mix only enough to dampen the dry ingredients.

Spoon batter into muffin pan cups, filling each ⅔ full.

Bake for approximately 20-25 minutes or until a toothpick inserted in the center comes out clean and dry. Remove from oven and cool in pan for 10 minutes. Turn out and allow to cool completely.

Yield: 12 muffins

Blue Corn Muffins: Substitute blue cornmeal for the yellow corn meal (it is available in most gourmet specialty shops).

Better Bran Muffins

This is a tasty way to meet your dietary fiber needs.

3 cups bran flakes cereal
1¼ cups all-purpose flour
½ cup sugar
1¼ teaspoons baking soda
¼ teaspoon salt
1 egg
1¾ cups buttermilk
¼ cup oil

Preheat oven to 400°. Grease muffin pan or prepare with liners.

In a large bowl, combine bran, flour, sugar, baking soda and salt. Add the egg, buttermilk and oil. Mix together briefly, just enough to moisten dry ingredients.

Spoon batter into muffin cups until ⅔ full.

Bake for approximately 20-25 minutes or until a toothpick inserted into the center comes out clean and dry. Remove from oven and cool for 10 minutes before turning out of pan.

Yield: 12 muffins

Raisin Bran Muffins: Add ½ cup raisins to the basic batter.

Whole Wheat Muffins

If you like whole wheat bread, you'll enjoy these muffins, which are light in texture and taste.

$3/4$ cup all-purpose flour
1 cup whole wheat flour
$1/4$ cup sugar
4 teaspoons baking powder
$1/2$ teaspoon salt
1 cup milk
1 egg
$1^1/4$ cup melted butter or oil

Preheat oven to 400°. Grease muffin pan or prepare with liners.

In a large bowl, whisk together the white and wheat flours, sugar, baking powder and salt. Add milk, egg and butter and mix just enough to moisten the dry ingredients.

Spoon batter into muffin cups about ⅔ full.

Bake for approximately 20-25 minutes or until a toothpick inserted into the center comes out clean and dry. Remove from oven and cool for 10 minutes before turning out of pan.

Yield: 12 muffins

Raisin or Peanut Whole Wheat Muffins: Add ¼ cup raisins or ¼ cup chopped peanuts to the batter.

Muffins from "The Big Apple"

This recipe, from The Little Pie Company of New York, is contributed by the owner, Arnold Wilkerson and his mother. The muffins taste great as is, but you can jazz them up with any of the suggested variations.

- 2 cups all-purpose flour
- 1/2 cup sugar
- 1 Tablespoon baking powder
- 1/2 teaspoon salt
- 1/2 cup butter, cut up into small pieces
- 2 eggs, beaten
- 1/2 cup sour cream
- 3/4 cup milk

Preheat oven to 425°. Grease muffin tin with vegetable shortening.

In a large mixing bowl, whisk together the flour, sugar, baking powder and salt.

Add butter and stir with a fork until flour has a grainy texture.

Add eggs, sour cream and milk to flour mixture and fold together.

Pour batter into muffin cups about 2/3 full and bake for approximately 15-20 minutes or until a toothpick inserted into the center comes out clean and dry. Remove from oven and let cool for 10 minutes before turning out.

Yield: 12 muffins

Walnut Raisin Muffins: Add 1/2 cup chopped walnuts and 1/2 cup raisins to batter and bake as above.

Apple Muffins: Add 1 cup peeled, chopped apple to batter and bake as above.

Sweet Topping for Muffins: Combine 2 tablespoons sugar and 1/4 teaspoon cinnamon and sprinkle on top of muffins before baking.

Popovers

These popovers are light and fluffy and are best served right from the oven. Serve with butter, jams or other sweet or savory spreads.

$1^1/4$ *cups all-purpose flour*
 $^1/4$ *teaspoon salt*
   3 *large eggs*
$1^1/4$ *cups milk*
   1 *Tablespoon unsalted butter, melted*
   2 *Tablespoons unsalted butter, cut into 6 even pieces*

Preheat oven to 400° and set rack in middle of oven. Grease a popover pan. Preheat popover pan in oven for about 2 minutes.

Blend flour, salt, eggs, milk and melted butter until mixture is the consistency of heavy cream, about 1-2 minutes. (The batter can be mixed in a food processor, blender, electric mixer or with a hand mixer.)

Place one small piece of butter in each cup and place pans back in preheated oven until butter is bubbly, about one minute. Fill each cup ½ full with batter and bake 20 minutes. Reduce temperature to 300° and continue baking 20 minutes.

Note: The batter can be made ahead of time and stored in the refrigerator, however the batter should be brought to room temperature before using.

Yield: 6 popovers

Dressed Up Muffins

Outrageous Blueberry Muffins

Add the blueberries individually to each muffin cup instead of into the batter bowl. This stops the berries from breaking and "bleeding" into the batter. I use a whole pint of blueberries because I love fresh fruit. Make sure to thoroughly dry the blueberries after rinsing them, or there will be too much liquid in the batter.

2¼ cups cake flour
1½ cups granulated sugar
¾ cup solid shortening
¾ cup milk
2 eggs
4 teaspoons double acting baking powder
1 teaspoon salt
1 teaspoon vanilla extract
1 pint (16 ounces) fresh blueberries (if using frozen, drain and dry)

Preheat oven to 375°. Grease and flour muffin cups or line with papers.

In a large mixing bowl, combine flour, sugar, shortening, milk, eggs, baking powder, salt and vanilla. Using an electric mixer, blend at low speed for about 2 minutes or until batter is smooth.

Spoon batter into muffin pan cups, filling each ⅔ full. Add 6-10 blueberries to the batter in each cup, mixing in several and leaving some at top.

Bake approximately 20-25 minutes or until a toothpick inserted in the center comes out clean and dry. Remove from oven and cool in pan for 10 minutes, then turn out and allow muffins to cool completely.

Yield: 16 muffins

Blueberry Muffins with Crumb Topping

This crumb topping is a delicious addition to the basic blueberry muffin recipe on page 15.

$1/2$ cup all-purpose flour
$1/2$ cup granulated sugar
1   teaspoon ground cinnamon
$1/4$ cup unsalted butter, softened
1   recipe Outrageous Blueberry Muffins, page 15

Preheat oven to 375°. Grease muffin cups or line with papers.

In a bowl, mix flour, sugar, cinnamon and butter together with a fork.

Prepare Blueberry Muffin batter as directed on page 15.

Spoon prepared batter into muffin pan cups, filling each ⅔ full. Add 6-10 blueberries to the batter in each cup. Sprinkle a tablespoon of the topping on each muffin. Add more berries on top of the crumbs.

Bake approximately 20-25 minutes or until a toothpick inserted in the center comes out clean and dry. Remove from oven and cool in pan for 10 minutes, then turn out and allow muffins to cool completely.

Yield: 16 muffins

Fruit Muffins: Instead of blueberries, use an equivalent amount of raspberries, blackberries, chopped strawberries (use ¼ cup less sugar in the batter), mixed berries, mulberries, or red currants (use ¼ cup more sugar in batter).

Applesauce-Blueberry Muffins

This is one of the wonderful creations of The Little Pie Company of New York. They graciously allowed us to print the outstanding recipe that follows.

    2   cups all-purpose flour
    1/2 cup sugar
    1   Tablespoon baking powder
    1/2 teaspoon salt
    1/2 cup cold unsalted butter, cut into small pieces
    2   eggs, beaten
    1/2 cup applesauce
    1   cup blueberries, washed, drained and patted dry

Preheat oven to 425°. Grease muffin tins or line with papers.

In a mixing bowl, combine flour, sugar, baking powder and salt. Add butter, and blend until mixture is grainy in texture.

In a small bowl, combine eggs and applesauce. Add to flour mixture and blend until ingredients are damp. Gently fold in the blueberries.

Pour batter into muffin cups about ⅔ full. Bake for about 15-20 minutes or until a toothpick inserted in the center comes out clean and dry. Remove from oven and let cool in pan for 10 minutes before turning out.

Yield: 12 muffins

Strawberry Raisin Muffins

These muffins go well with brunch and they have a lovely pink hue from the strawberries. If you use frozen strawberries, drain well and pat dry with paper towels before using.

4 eggs
1 1/2 cups sugar
2 cups fresh strawberries, cut in half
1 1/2 cups raisins
1/2 cup butter, melted
3 cups all-purpose flour
1/4 teaspoon salt
1 1/2 teaspoons baking powder
3/4 teaspoon cinnamon

Preheat oven to 350°. Grease and flour muffin tins or line with papers.

In a bowl, combine eggs, sugar, strawberries, raisins and butter.

Stir together flour, salt, baking powder and cinnamon. Stir dry ingredients into strawberry mixture until just moistened; batter will be thick. Do not over-mix. Divide batter evenly into muffin cups.

Bake for approximately 20-25 minutes or until a toothpick inserted in the center comes out clean and dry. Remove from oven and allow to cool in pan for 10 minutes before turning out.

Yield: 24 muffins

Cranberry Apple Muffins

These muffins are absolutely delicious. Try cutting them in half and topping them with a big scoop of vanilla ice cream.

2   *MacIntosh apples (or other baking apples)*
1   *Tablespoon cinnamon*
2   *Tablespoons plus 2 cups sugar, divided*
3   *cups all-purpose flour*
4   *teaspoons baking powder*
1   *teaspoon salt*
1   *cup oil*
4   *eggs, beaten*
³/₄ *cup cranberry juice*
3   *teaspoons vanilla*
1   *cup whole fresh cranberries*
3   *ounces coarsely chopped walnuts, optional*

Preheat oven to 375°. Grease muffin pans or line with papers.

Peel and core apples; cut into small pieces. Place apples in a bowl and sprinkle with cinnamon and two tablespoons sugar. Mix and set aside.

In a large mixing bowl, whisk together the flour, baking powder and salt.

In another bowl, combine the oil, eggs, cranberry juice, vanilla, cranberries and 2 cups sugar. Stir wet mixture into the flour mixture, stirring ingredients until just moistened. Add walnuts if desired.

Spoon batter into muffin cups approximately ⅓ full. Place a tablespoon of the apple mixture into each muffin cup, then fill the remainder of the muffin cup (almost to top) with additional batter.

Bake for approximately 20-25 minutes or until toothpick inserted into the center comes out clean and dry. Remove from oven and let cool for 10 minutes.

Yield: 24 muffins

Banana Nut Muffins

This recipe is a great way to use up your overripe bananas.

1/2 cup unsalted butter, at room temperature
1 1/2 cups granulated sugar
2 cups mashed bananas (about 4 medium)
2 eggs, beaten
1/2 cup buttermilk
2 1/2 cups all-purpose flour
1 teaspoon baking soda
1/2 teaspoon baking powder
1/4 teaspoon salt
1/4 cup chopped walnuts

Preheat oven to 375°. Grease and flour muffin pans or line with papers.

In a large mixing bowl, combine butter and sugar until thoroughly blended. Stir in banana, eggs and buttermilk.

In another bowl, whisk together the flour, baking soda, baking powder and salt. Stir wet ingredients into the dry, mixing until dry ingredients are moistened. Blend in walnuts.

Spoon batter into muffin pan cups until 2/3 full.

Bake for 15-20 minutes or until a toothpick inserted in the center comes out clean and dry. Remove from oven and allow to cool in pan for 10 minutes before turning out.

Yield: 18 muffins

Chocolate-Banana Muffins

This delectable muffin recipe is contributed by the Muffins n' Cream Bakery and Restaurant in Coeur d'Alene, Idaho.

   2   cups mashed banana (about 4 medium)
   1   egg
   1/3   cup vegetable oil
   1 1/4   cups sugar
   1/3   cup water
   1/3   cup unsweetened cocoa powder
   2   cups all-purpose flour
   1   teaspoon baking soda
   1/2   teaspoon baking powder
   1/4   teaspoon nutmeg
   1/4   teaspoon salt
   1/2   teaspoon cinnamon

Preheat oven to 375°. Grease and flour muffin pan or line with papers.

In a blender, combine bananas, egg, oil, sugar and water.

In a large bowl, whisk together the cocoa, flour, baking soda, baking powder, nutmeg, salt and cinnamon.

Stir wet mixture into dry ingredients, mixing only until combined.

Spoon batter into muffin cups 2/3 full and bake for 20-25 minutes or until a toothpick inserted into the center comes out clean and dry. Remove from oven and let cool in pan for 10 minutes before turning out.

Yield: 12 muffins

Banana-Chocolate Chip Muffins

If you like bananas and chocolate, you'll love this yummy combination.

> 1 cup sugar
> 1 egg
> 1/2 cup butter, at room temperature
> 1 cup mashed ripe bananas (about 2 medium)
> 3 Tablespoons milk
> 2 cups all-purpose flour
> 2 teaspoons baking powder
> 1 cup chocolate chips
> 1 cup chopped walnuts

Preheat oven to 325°. Grease and flour muffin pans or line with papers.

In a mixing bowl, cream together the sugar, egg and butter.

In another bowl, combine mashed bananas and milk.

Whisk together the flour and baking powder. Stir dry ingredients into the sugar mixture. Add banana mixture and blend until just combined. Fold in chocolate chips and walnuts.

Spoon batter into muffin cups ⅔ full. Bake for 25-30 minutes or until a toothpick inserted into the center comes out clean and dry. (When testing, don't confuse the melted chocolate with moist muffin. Try to do the toothpick test without hitting a chocolate chip.)

Remove from oven and let cool in pan for 10 minutes before turning out.

Yield: 12 muffins

Macadamia and White Chocolate Muffins

Make sure to chop the macadamia nuts — they are very hard to chew otherwise!

- 2 cups all-purpose flour
- 4 teaspoons baking powder
- 1 teaspoon salt
- 1 cup granulated sugar
- 1/2 cup unsalted butter, melted
- 2 eggs, beaten
- 1 cup milk
- 1 cup macadamia nuts, coarsely chopped
- 1 cup white chocolate chips or chunks

Preheat oven to 400°. Grease muffin pans or line with papers.

In a mixing bowl, combine the flour, baking powder, salt and sugar.

In another bowl, combine the melted butter, beaten eggs and milk. Stir wet ingredients into the dry ingredients, combing only enough to moisten. Mix in macadamia nuts and white chocolate chips.

Spoon batter into paper liners ¾ full. Bake for approximately 18-20 minutes or until a toothpick inserted in the center comes out clean and dry. Remove from oven and cool for 10 minutes before turning out of pan.

Yield: 12 muffins

The Everything Muffin

This muffin is candy-like in its taste and texture. Add any combination of raisins, nuts and chips you prefer, but don't exceed a total of 2½ cups added ingredients.

- 2 cups all-purpose flour
- 4 teaspoons baking powder
- 1 teaspoon salt
- 1 cup granulated sugar
- ½ cup unsalted butter, melted
- 2 eggs, beaten
- 1 cup milk
- ½ cup light raisins
- ½ cup dark raisins
- ½ cup chopped walnuts, pecans or cashews
- ½ cup semisweet chocolate chips
- ½ cup peanut butter or butterscotch chips

Preheat oven to 400°. Grease muffin pans or line with papers.

In a mixing bowl, whisk together the flour, baking powder, salt and sugar.

In another bowl, combine the melted butter, beaten eggs and milk. Stir wet ingredients into the dry ingredients, combing only enough to moisten. Mix in the raisins, nuts and chips (don't exceed a total of 2½ cups added ingredients).

Fill each muffin cup about ¾ full. Bake for approximately 18-20 minutes or until a toothpick inserted into the center comes out clean and dry. Remove from oven and cool for 10 minutes before turning out of pan.

Yield: 12 muffins

Sour Cream Coffee Cake Muffins

Served warm, these muffins make a good breakfast treat or coffee break snack.

    1   cup unsalted butter, at room temperature
    1   cup granulated sugar
    4   eggs
    1   cup sour cream
  2¹/4 cups cake flour
    1   Tablespoon baking powder
    1   teaspoon baking soda
  ¹/2   teaspoon salt

Topping Mixture:

  ¹/2   cup granulated sugar
  ¹/2   cup all-purpose flour
    2   teaspoons cinnamon
  ¹/4   cup unsalted butter, softened

Preheat oven to 375°. Grease and flour muffin pans or line with papers.

In the bowl of an electric mixer, combine butter, sugar, eggs, and sour cream. Beat at high speed until smooth.

In another mixing bowl, whisk together the flour, baking powder, baking soda and salt.

In a small bowl, combine sugar, flour, cinnamon and butter for topping, mixing together with a fork until crumbly. Set aside.

Gradually combine the dry muffin ingredients into the sour cream mixture and beat at low speed until ingredients are dampened. Turn to high and beat until batter is smooth. Fill each muffin pan with batter ⅔ full. Sprinkle a little topping mixture on each muffin.

Bake for approximately 20-25 minutes or until a toothpick inserted in the center comes out clean and dry. Remove from oven and cool for approximately 10 minutes before turning out of pan.

Yield: 18 muffins

Spicy Cheddar Muffins

Black olives add an interesting flavor to these muffins from the Muffins n' Cream Bakery and Restaurant in Coeur d'Alene, Idaho. They go well with a bowl of chili.

4	cups all-purpose flour
1/2	cup cheddar cheese, grated
1/4	cup black olives, chopped
1	Tablespoon baking powder
1/2	teaspoon garlic salt
1/2	teaspoon chili powder
1/4	teaspoon cayenne powder
2	eggs, beaten
1/4	cup vegetable oil
1 1/4	cups milk

Preheat oven to 375°. Grease and flour the muffin pans or line with papers.

In a mixing bowl, combine the flour, cheese, olives, baking powder, garlic salt, chili powder and cayenne powder.

In another bowl, combine the eggs, oil and milk. Stir the wet ingredients into the dry mix and blend until just combined.

Spoon batter into muffin pan cups about ⅔ full. Bake for 20-25 minutes or until a toothpick inserted in the center comes out clean and dry. Remove from oven and let cool in pan for 10 minutes before turning out.

Yield: 24 muffins

Hot and Spicy Jalapeño Muffins

These muffins are hot and spicy! But if you find that they are just not hot enough for your taste, next time add some extra jalapeño peppers, 1/4 teaspoon hot cayenne pepper or 1-2 dashes of tabasco.

1 1/4   *cups all-purpose flour*
  3   *teaspoons baking powder*
  1   *teaspoon salt*
  2   *Tablespoons sugar*
 3/4   *cup yellow cornmeal*
  2   *eggs, beaten lightly*
  1   *cup milk*
 1/4   *cup sweet butter, melted*
  4   *fresh jalapeño peppers, seeded and diced*
 1/4   *teaspoon dried crushed cayenne pepper*
  1   *cup grated pepperjack or mozzarella cheese*

Preheat oven to 375°. Grease and flour muffin pan or line with papers.

In a mixing bowl, whisk together the flour, baking powder, salt, sugar and cornmeal.

In another bowl, combine the eggs, milk, butter, jalapeño peppers and cayenne pepper. Stir wet mixture into the dry, mixing just enough to dampen the dry ingredients.

Spoon batter into muffin pan cups about 2/3 way full.

Bake for 20-25 minutes or until a toothpick inserted in the center comes out clean and dry. Remove from oven.

Sprinkle cheese on top of muffins. Place pan in oven for an additional 3-4 minutes, then remove from oven and allow to cool in pan for 10 minutes. Serve hot.

Yield: 12 muffins

Broccoli and Cheese Muffins

These muffins make an attractive luncheon dish. Serve with soup and dessert for a complete meal.

21 *broccoli florets, steamed and cooled*
4 *cups all purpose flour*
1/4 *cup sugar*
4 *teaspoons baking powder*
1 *teaspoon salt*
2 *cups milk*
2 *eggs*
1/2 *cup oil*
3/4 *cup shredded cheddar cheese, plus 1/4 cup for garnish*

Preheat oven to 400°. Grease and flour muffin pans or line with papers.

Chop 3 broccoli florets into tiny pieces. Reserve the remaining broccoli for later.

In a large bowl, whisk together flour, sugar, baking powder and salt.

In another bowl, combine milk, eggs and oil. Stir wet mixture into dry ingredients, mixing just enough to moisten the dry ingredients.

Add the chopped broccoli and 3/4 cup shredded cheddar cheese to the batter and mix gently by hand. Batter will be lumpy. Spoon batter into pans about 2/3 full.

Bake for approximately 20-25 minutes or until toothpick inserted in the center comes out clean and dry.

Remove muffins from the oven. Insert a broccoli floret into the top of each muffin. Sprinkle remaining cheddar cheese on tops of muffins and place muffin pan back into oven for approximately 2-3 minutes, or until cheese melts. Remove from oven and serve warm.

Hint: Add a teaspoon of sugar to the water while you steam the broccoli to keep the florets bright green in color.

Yield: 12 muffins

Stuffin' Muffins

Basic Stuffin' Muffin

The Stuffin' Muffin is an oversized popover-style muffin that can be filled with a variety of stuffings or fillings to make a great lunch or dinner dish. Why have a plain muffin when you can "go stuff it" instead?

    6 eggs
    2 cups milk
    2 tablespoons unsalted butter, melted and cooled
    2 cups all-purpose flour
    1 teaspoon salt

Preheat oven to 375°. Grease six 10-ounce ramekins (4 inch size).

In the bowl of an electric mixer, beat eggs for 3 minutes on low speed. Gradually add milk and butter.

Continue beating, still on low speed, while adding the flour and salt. Beat on high speed for 3 minutes.

Pour batter into ramekins, filling about ½ full. Bake for 30 minutes, then lower heat to 325° and bake for another 30 minutes, or until muffins are a deep golden brown. (Do not open the oven door during the first 45 minutes of baking or the muffins may collapse!)

Remove muffins from oven and pierce each one with a knife so steam can escape.

Yield: 6 stuffin' muffins

HOW TO STUFF A MUFFIN

To stuff the muffins, gently remove them from the ramekins. Slice off the tops with a sharp knife. Fill each muffin with the stuffing of your choice (see the recipes and stuffing ideas on the next two pages). Place the muffin tops back on, or leave the tops off and overstuff the muffins, mounding the filling on the top. For hot fillings, place the filled muffins on a baking sheet and warm for 10 minutes at 300°.

Crab Meat Stuffing

Use this filling in the Basic Stuffin' Muffin. Served by candlelight with a fine wine, this becomes the basis for an elegant meal.

1 *pound lump crab meat*
1 *egg, beaten*
  salt and pepper, to taste
6 *sprigs parsley, chopped*
3 *Tablespoons parmesan or romano cheese*
3 *Tablespoons chopped celery*
1 *Tablespoons butter*

Rinse and drain crab meat and place in a bowl. Add egg, salt and pepper, chopped parsley and cheese. Stir to combine.

In a saucepan over medium heat, sauté the celery in 1 tablespoon butter until soft. Add crab meat mixture and cook over low heat for 3-5 minutes, stirring, until egg is set.

Slice tops off muffins. Spoon filling inside and replace tops. Place filled muffins on a baking sheet and heat at 300° for about 10 minutes.

Yield: Filling for six stuffin' muffins

Sausage, Pepper & Onion Stuffing

Use this filling in the Basic Stuffin' Muffin. This Italian-style stuffing is sure to become a favorite.

    4   links Italian sausage, sweet or hot
   1/3 cup butter
    1   green pepper, seeded and chopped
    1   red pepper, seeded and chopped
    1   yellow pepper, seeded and chopped
    1   medium onion, chopped
        salt and pepper, to taste

Place sausage links in a small baking pan and pierce each one 2-3 times with a fork. Bake at 350° for 30 minutes, or until fully cooked. Cool, then chop into small pieces.

In a skillet over medium heat, melt the butter. Sauté the peppers and onion in the butter for 5 minutes, or until tender. Add chopped, cooked sausage and stir to combine. Season with salt and pepper, to taste.

Slice tops off muffins. Spoon filling inside and replace tops. Place filled muffins on a baking sheet and heat at 300° for about 10 minutes.

Yield: Filling for six stuffin' muffins

Broccoli & Cheese Stuffing

Put a teaspoon of sugar in the water while you steam the broccoli to keep the florets bright green in color.

12-18 broccoli florets
1 cup grated cheddar cheese

Steam the broccoli florets just until bright green and tender. Drain well.

Slice tops off muffins. Place two florets inside each one, heap cheddar cheese on top of the broccoli, and replace tops. Place filled muffins on a baking sheet and heat at 300° for about 10 minutes.

Yield: Filling for six stuffin' muffins

Mashed Potato Stuffing

Use this filling in the Basic Stuffin' Muffin. This makes a nice side dish instead of serving regular mashed or baked potatoes.

   3   *Tablespoons butter*
   1   *medium onion, coarsely chopped*
   3   *large potatoes, peeled and chopped*
        salt and pepper, to taste

In a skillet over medium heat, melt the butter. Sauté the onion in the butter for about 5 minutes, or until tender. Set aside.

Place the peeled, chopped potatoes in a large pot and cover with salted water. Bring to a boil and cook until potatoes are tender. Drain off water and mash the potatoes. Stir in the cooked onion and season with salt and pepper, to taste. Thin with warm milk, if necessary.

Slice tops off muffins. Spoon filling inside and replace tops. Place filled muffins on a baking sheet and heat at 300° for about 10 minutes.

Yield: Filling for six stuffin' muffins

Other Stuffing Ideas

Use your imagination to create new fillings for the Basic Stuffin' Muffin. Here are a few suggestions to get you started:

   Cold chicken salad
   Hot chicken pot pie filling
   Cold crab salad topped with chopped tomato and bacon
   Tuna salad
   Lobster salad topped with shredded cheese
   Hot chili, chopped onions and shredded cheese
   Shrimp creole
   Egg salad
   Hot spinach soufflé
   Corned beef hash
   Scrambled eggs, chopped ham and shredded cheese

Cupcakes
Plain & Fancy

Chocolate Peanut Butter Cupcakes

Your kids will love these chocolate cupcakes filled with creamy peanut butter—and so will you!

2	cups cake flour
1³/4	cups granulated sugar
³/4	cup cocoa
1¹/4	cups milk
³/4	cup solid shortening
3	eggs
1¹/4	teaspoons baking soda
1	teaspoon baking powder
1	cup peanut butter chips
1	jar (16 ounces) smooth peanut butter

Preheat oven to 350°. Grease and flour cupcake pans or line with papers.

In a large bowl of an electric mixer, combine all ingredients except peanut butter chips and peanut butter. Using a mixer, blend at low speed until moistened, scrape sides of bowl and mix at high speed for 2 minutes. Stir in peanut butter chips by hand.

Spoon batter into muffin pans, filling each ²/3 full. Bake for approximately 20-25 minutes or until a toothpick inserted in the center comes out clean and dry. Remove from oven and cool in pan for 10 minutes before turning out. Cool completely after removing from pan.

Place room temperature peanut butter into a 12-inch size pastry bag with a #12 open tip (¹/4-inch). Gently push tip into center of each cupcake and squeeze the bag until peanut butter reaches the top of cupcake. Remove pastry tip from cupcake and repeat with other cupcakes. Ice with chocolate icing, if desired.

Hint: Chunky peanut butter will clog the pastry tip. Make sure to use smooth peanut butter at room temperature.

Yield: 24 cupcakes

Holiday Fruit & Nut Cupcakes

These cupcakes make nice holiday gifts. They can be made in advance and stored in the freezer. To store, wrap cupcakes in cheese cloth saturated with rum or in saran wrap and then again in aluminum foil.

Batter:

3/4	cup unsalted butter
	juice of 1 lemon
3/4	cup brown sugar
3	eggs
3	Tablespoons dark rum
1	cup all-purpose flour
1/2	teaspoon baking powder
1/2	teaspoon ground cinnamon
1/2	teaspoon powdered cloves

Fruits and Nuts:

1	cup diced candied fruit
1/2	cup light raisins
1/2	cup dark raisins
1/4	cup currants
1/4	cup dried apricots, chopped
1/4	cup red and green candied pineapple, chopped
1/4	cup blanched almonds
1/4	cup chopped walnuts
1/4	cup chopped pecans

Preheat oven to 350°. Line cupcake pans with papers.

Cream together the butter, lemon juice and brown sugar. Stir in the eggs, rum, flour, baking powder, cinnamon and cloves; mix until creamy. Blend in fruits and nuts. Spoon batter into cups to top of papers. Bake for 45-60 minutes.

Remove from pan, and brush top of cupcakes with dark rum. Wrap fruit cupcakes in cheese cloth or saran wrap and aluminum foil and freeze.

Yield: 48 cupcakes

Chocolate Cupcakes

Ice these cupcakes with chocolate glaze, butter cream frosting, lemon frosting or cream cheese frosting.

2	ounces semisweet chocolate chips
1	teaspoon instant coffee
1	cup boiling water
2	cups all purpose flour
1	teaspoon baking soda
1	teaspoon baking powder
1/8	teaspoon salt
1/2	cup unsalted butter, room temperature
1/2	teaspoon vanilla extract
1 3/4	cups light brown sugar
2	eggs (extra large)
1/4	cup sour cream

Preheat oven to 325°. Grease and flour cupcake pans or line with papers.

In a saucepan, place chocolate chips, instant coffee and water, stirring constantly at medium heat until chocolate melts. Remove from heat and allow to cool.

In the bowl of an electric mixer, combine the flour, baking soda, baking powder, salt, butter, vanilla and brown sugar. Beat for half a minute on low speed and then gradually add eggs, sour cream and the chocolate mixture. Blend at high speed for 3 minutes. Scrape the sides of the bowl and beat for another 2 minutes. Spoon batter into each cupcake well, about ⅔ full.

Bake for approximately 30-35 minutes or until a toothpick inserted in the center comes out clean and dry. Remove from oven and let cool in pan for 10 minutes before turning out.

Yield: 24 cupcakes

Black Forest Cupcakes

These rich chocolate cupcakes are miniature versions of Black Forest Cake, complete with whipped cream and cherry filling. They are a little messy, so make these a plate-and-fork dessert.

1 recipe Chocolate Cupcakes, page 41
1 cup heavy cream
1/4 pound semisweet chocolate
1 can (8 ounces) sweet dark pitted cherries, drained and patted dry

Make Chocolate Cupcakes as directed on page 38. (Grease and flour the cupcake pans—do not use paper liners since you will be cutting these cupcakes into thirds.)

In the bowl of an electric mixer, place heavy cream. Beat at high speed until cream is stiff (do not overbeat).

To make chocolate shavings, place chocolate in a warm place for 30 minutes. Using a potato peeler, shave chocolate in one direction to form chocolate curls.

Using a serrated knife, gently cut cupcakes in thirds. On the bottom third, place a layer of cherries. Place middle cupcake layer on top of cherries. Spread with whipped cream. Place top third of cupcake on top of whipped cream. Decorate with whipped cream and chocolate shavings.

Note: you can substitute chocolate jimmies or sprinkles for the shaved chocolate.

Yield: 24 cupcakes

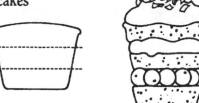

Carrot Cupcakes

I prefer to use shredded rather than grated carrots in this recipe. Shredded carrots retain their color and taste better than the grated, and give these cupcakes their distinctive flavor and texture. Ice with the Cream Cheese Icing on page 56.

2	cups sugar
1¹/₂	cups oil
3	cups all-purpose flour
2	teaspoons baking powder
2	teaspoons baking soda
2	teaspoons cinnamon
¹/₂	teaspoon salt
4	eggs
2	cups shredded carrots
1	teaspoon vanilla extract

Preheat oven to 425°. Grease cupcake pans or line with papers.

In a large bowl, mix all the ingredients until thoroughly blended.

Spoon batter into cups until ⅔ full.

Bake for 20-25 minutes or until a toothpick inserted in the center comes out clean and dry. Remove from oven and allow cupcakes to cool completely before icing.

Carrot Raisin Nut Cupcakes: Add 1 cup dark raisins, 1 cup light raisins and 1 cup coarse chopped walnuts to the batter.

Yield: 24 cupcakes

Cream Cheese Cupcakes

Most everyone loves cheesecake, but in my family we all like different toppings. That's why I took the family recipe and turned it into cupcakes. I use a variety of toppings or fillings and satisfy everyone. Here is the basic recipe, followed by suggestions for toppings and variations on the next four pages.

Crust:

$1^{1}/2$ cups graham cracker crumbs
$^{1}/2$ cup butter, melted
$^{1}/2$ cup granulated sugar
1   teaspoon ground cinnamon
1   teaspoon ground ginger

Filling:

3   8-ounce packages cream cheese, softened
1   cup granulated sugar
$^{1}/8$ teaspoon salt
4   eggs
2   Tablespoons vanilla extract

Preheat oven to 350°. Line cupcake pans with papers.

To make the crust, mix graham cracker crumbs, butter, sugar, cinnamon and ginger with a fork until moist. Spoon one tablespoon of mixture into each lined cup and press down (you may have some crust mixture left over).

To make filling, place the cream cheese, sugar, salt, eggs, and vanilla into the bowl of an electric mixer. Beat at high speed until smooth and creamy. Spoon filling mixture into each cup, about ⅔ way full.

Bake for approximately 30-35 minutes or until toothpick inserted in the center comes out clean and dry. Remove from oven and cool in pan for 10-15 minutes. Add toppings and refrigerate until ready to serve.

Yield: 36 cupcakes

Sour Cream Topping

Prepare the Cream Cheese Cupcakes on page 41. Then top with this sour cream layer and finish baking.

    1¹/2 cups sour cream
      4   Tablespoons sugar
      2   teaspoons vanilla extract

In a bowl, combine the sour cream, sugar and vanilla.

Bake cupcakes for approximately 25-30 minutes, remove from oven and spoon the sour cream mixture on top of each cupcake.

Bake an additional 10 minutes at 350°. Remove from oven, let cool as directed and then refrigerate until serving time.

Pineapple Topping

Prepare the Cream Cheese Cupcakes on page 41. Then top with this pineapple topping for a tropical treat.

> 1   *16-ounce can crushed pineapple, drained, reserve juice*
>   *water, as needed*
> *3/4* *cup granulated sugar*
> 3   *Tablespoons cornstarch*
> 2   *Tablespoons flour*
> 2   *egg yolks*

Pour reserved pineapple juice into a 2-cup measure. Add enough water to equal a total of 1⅓ cups liquid.

In a saucepan, combine the sugar, cornstarch and flour. Add pineapple juice-water mixture, and cook over medium high heat until heated. Reduce to low flame, and cook until thick, stirring frequently. Add egg yolks and cook another 2 minutes. Stir in crushed pineapple.

Mandarin Orange-Pineapple Topping

> 1   *8-ounce can crushed pineapple, drained, reserve juice*
> 1   *11-ounce can Mandarin oranges, drained, reserve juice*
>   *water, as needed*
> *3/4* *cup granulated sugar*
> 3   *Tablespoons cornstarch*
> 2   *Tablespoons flour*
> 2   *egg yolks*

Pour reserved pineapple and Mandarin orange juice into a 2-cup measure. Add enough water to equal a total of 1⅓ cups liquid. Chop the Mandarin oranges into small pieces. Set aside.

In a saucepan, combine the sugar, cornstarch and flour. Add the juice-water mixture, and cook over medium high heat until heated. Reduce to low flame, and cook until thick, stirring frequently. Add egg yolks and cook another 2 minutes. Stir in crushed pineapple and chopped Mandarin oranges.

Cranberry Topping

Prepare the Cream Cheese Cupcakes on page 41. Then top with this cranberry topping. (Hint: keep the pan covered, otherwise the cranberries may splash out and stain the kitchen counters.)

   2   cups cranberries
   1½   cups granulated sugar
   6   ounces cranberry juice concentrate
        grated rind of 1 orange

   In saucepan, place cranberries, sugar, cranberry juice concentrate and orange rind. Cover and boil until berries start to pop. Strain the berries, reserving the juice to use in the Cranberry Glaze, if desired. Mash the berries and spoon on top of each cupcake.

   Cranberry Glaze: Add 2 tablespoons orange liqueur to ¼ cup of reserved juice to make a glaze. Brush on top of cupcakes, then top with fruit.

Cream Cheese Cupcake Variations

Any of the following variations or toppings go well with the Cream Cheese Cupcakes on page 41.

Chocolate Chip Cheesecake: Add 4 ounces of mini chocolate chips to the cream cheese filling before baking.

Chocolate Cheesecake: On top of a double boiler, melt 4 ounces of semisweet chocolate. Mix into the cream cheese filling before baking.

Chocolate Covered Cheesecake: On top of double boiler, melt 2 ounces of chocolate and pour over tops of cupcakes after baked and cooled.

Fresh Fruit Cheesecake: Thinly slice your favorite fresh fruit. Make a glaze from one cup of water or fruit liqueur and one (¼-ounce) package of unflavored gelatin. Soften the gelatin in ¼ cup of the water or liqueur, then add the rest of liquid. Bring to a boil and cool. Arrange fresh fruit on top of cupcakes and spoon a little glaze over the fruit. Refrigerate for two hours before serving.

Liqueur and Fresh Fruit Combinations:
- Midori Liqueur with honeydew melon balls
- Midori Liqueur with kiwis and strawberries
- Grand Marnier with Mandarin oranges or peaches
- Apricot brandy with canned apricots
- Chamborg with fresh raspberries

Carrot and Raisin Cupcakes

This recipe calls for brown sugar, molasses and whole wheat flour which give the cupcakes a robust flavor.

2 cups unbleached flour
1 cup whole wheat flour
1/3 cup sugar
1/3 cup non-instant powdered milk
2 Tablespoons baking powder
1 1/2 teaspoons salt
1/4 cup dark brown sugar
1/4 cup raisins
2 carrots, grated (3/4 cup)
1/4 cup molasses
2 eggs
1/4 cup vegetable oil
2 cups water

Preheat oven to 350°. Grease and flour cupcake pans or line with papers.

In a mixing bowl, combine unbleached and whole wheat flour, sugar, powdered milk, baking powder and salt. Add brown sugar and raisins and mix thoroughly.

In another mixing bowl, combine carrots, molasses, eggs, vegetable oil and water. Add to the dry mixture. Blend only until mixed, do not over-mix.

Spoon batter into cupcake pan, filling each well about ⅔ full.

Bake for about 20-25 minutes or until a toothpick inserted into the center comes out clean and dry. Remove from oven and let cool for 10 minutes before turning out of pan.

Yield: 12 cupcakes

Pumpkin Cupcakes

For a Halloween treat, ice with chocolate frosting and pipe an orange pumpkin on top of each cupcake.

2¹/2 cups cake flour
1 Tablespoon baking powder
¹/2 teaspoon salt
¹/2 teaspoon cinnamon
¹/4 teaspoon nutmeg
¹/4 teaspoon ginger
1 Tablespoon pumpkin pie spice
¹/2 cup shortening
³/4 cup granulated sugar
³/4 cup light brown sugar
2 eggs
1 can (16 ounces) pumpkin
¹/2 cup milk

Preheat oven to 350°. Grease muffin pans or prepare with liners.

In a bowl, whisk together cake flour, baking powder, salt, cinnamon, nutmeg, ginger and pumpkin pie spice.

In bowl of an electric mixer, place shortening, granulated sugar, light brown sugar, eggs, pumpkin and milk. Mix together until smooth and creamy, then gradually combine the flour mixture into the pumpkin mixture. Beat at low speed until the ingredients are moistened, then switch to high speed until batter is smooth.

Spoon batter into cupcake pan, filling each well about ⅔ full.

Bake for about 20-25 minutes or until a toothpick inserted in the center comes out clean and dry. Remove from oven and cool for 10 minutes before turning out of pan.

Yield: 18 cupcakes

Apple Cupcakes

I like the taste of Winesap apples in this recipe, but you can use Cortland or MacIntosh if you wish. Serve them hot, split open, with a scoop of vanilla ice cream on top. Heavenly!

Apple Mixture

2	*Winesap apples*
1	*Tablespoon cinnamon*
2	*Tablespoons sugar*

Cupcake Batter

2	*cups sugar*
3	*cups all purpose flour*
4	*teaspoons baking powder*
1/2	*teaspoon salt*
1	*cup oil*
4	*eggs*
3/4	*cup orange juice*
3	*teaspoons vanilla*

Preheat oven to 375°. Grease cupcake pans or line with papers.

Peel, core and cut up apples into small pieces, and place into a bowl. Sprinkle cinnamon and sugar on the apples and stir to mix. Set aside.

In a mixing bowl, combine sugar, flour, baking powder and salt.

In another bowl, combine the oil, eggs, orange juice and vanilla. Fold wet ingredients into the dry, stirring until the mixture is smooth.

Spoon batter into cupcake pans, filling each well ⅓ full. Place a tablespoon of the apple mixture on top of the batter, then fill almost to the top of the pan with additional batter.

Bake for approximately 18-20 minutes or until a toothpick inserted in center comes out clean and dry.

Yield: 18 cupcakes

Yellow Cupcakes

These taste good with almost any flavor of icing or glaze.

3/4 cup sweet butter, melted
4 eggs
1/2 cup milk
2 teaspoons vanilla extract
2 cups sifted cake flour
2 cups sugar
1 teaspoon baking soda
2 teaspoons baking powder
1/2 teaspoon salt

Preheat oven to 350°. Grease and flour cupcake pans or line with papers.

In a mixing bowl, combine butter, eggs, milk and vanilla. Beat well at high speed. Add flour, sugar, baking soda, baking powder and salt to the wet ingredients and beat at low until ingredients are moistened, then at high until batter is completely smooth. Fill cupcake pan wells ⅔ full.

Bake for about 15-20 minutes or until a toothpick inserted in the center comes out clean and dry.

Remove from oven and allow to cool in pan for 10 minutes before turning out.

Yield: 18-24 cupcakes

Cranberry Charlotte Russe: Top cupcakes with the Cranberry Topping (page 44), and fresh whipped cream.

Fancy Fillings: You can fill yellow cupcakes with any of the toppings described on pages 42-45. Put toppings into a pastry bag with #4B tip. Insert tip into top of cupcake and squeeze until cupcake is filled. Or, cut cupcake in half and spread with topping.

Lemon with a Twist Cupcakes

These cupcakes are very light and delicious. You can substitute 2 teaspoons lemon extract for the lemon juice and lemon rind, if you prefer. Try them with Larry's Lemon Icing on page 55—it adds a real zing!

4½	cups all purpose flour
3	cups granulated sugar
1½	cups solid shortening
1½	cups milk
6	eggs
5	teaspoons double acting baking powder
1½	Tablespoons lemon juice
1	Tablespoon lemon rind

Preheat oven to 350°. Grease cupcake pans or line with papers.

In the bowl of an electric mixer, combine all ingredients. Mix at low, then at high as flour becomes moistened. Beat until batter is creamy, about 2 minutes Spoon batter into cups about ¾ full.

Bake for approximately 20-25 minutes or until a toothpick inserted in the center comes out clean and dry. Remove cupcakes from oven and allow to cool before icing.

Yield: 48 cupcakes

Honey Cupcakes

Add the cherries by hand after mixing the other ingredients so they won't break.

>   1 cup unsalted butter
>   1 cup clover honey
>   4 eggs
>   juice from ¹/₂ lemon
>   grated rind from ¹/₂ lemon
>   3 cups cake flour
>   2 teaspoons baking powder
>   ¹/₂ teaspoon salt
>   1 cup candied red cherries (optional),
>   cut into halves or quarters

Preheat oven to 350°. Grease cupcake pans or line with papers.

In the bowl of an electric mixer, cream the butter and honey at high speed. Add the eggs, lemon juice, and lemon rind. Beat until smooth. Gradually add the flour, baking powder and salt, and continue beating until smooth.

Add cherries and mix in gently with a fork. Spoon batter into cups until ¾ filled.

Bake for approximately 15-20 minutes or until a toothpick inserted into the center comes out clean and dry. Remove from oven and allow to cool 10 minutes before turning out of pan.

Variation: Add 1 cup chopped walnuts to the batter at the same time you add the cherries. For a less sweet muffin use ¾ cup honey instead of 1 cup.

Yield: 24 cupcakes

Chocolate Mousse Cupcakes

I like to serve these frozen mousse cupcakes as a dinner party dessert. They take a little time to prepare, but will draw raves from your family and friends. They are easiest to eat with a spoon.

Cookie Crust:

$1^{1}/2$ cups chocolate wafers, crushed
$^{1}/4$ cup sugar
$^{1}/4$ cup butter, melted

Mousse Filling:

$^{1}/2$ cup cold coffee, instant or brewed
$2^{1}/4$ cups granulated sugar, divided
12 1-ounce squares semisweet chocolate
3 $^{1}/4$-ounce packages unflavored gelatin
3 cups heavy cream

Line cupcake wells with heavy-duty foil liners.

In a bowl, combine cookie crumbs, sugar and melted butter. Place 1 to 2 tablespoons crumb mixture in the bottom of each cupcake paper and press down to form a crust.

In a heavy 2-quart saucepan, sprinkle one package gelatin over the coffee. Let rest 1 minute and stir to dissolve. Add ½ cup sugar and stir over low heat to dissolve. Add chocolate, and stir constantly until smooth. Remove from heat and let stand 5 minutes to cool slightly.

In a large bowl, sprinkle 2 packages gelatin over heavy cream. Let rest 1 minute and stir to dissolve. Beat whipped cream until it is stiff.

Fold half the chocolate mixture into the whipped cream, then fold in the rest of the chocolate mixture.

Spoon mousse into cupcake papers, filling to the top. Place the filled muffin pans into the freezer overnight, then finish decorating with the whipped cream topping and chocolate curls as explained on page 53.

Whipped Cream Topping

The Whip-It® or Dream Whip® is optional, but it will make the whipped cream stiffer and easier to pipe. If you can't find vanilla sugar in the baking section of your supermarket, make your own by placing a vanilla bean in 2 Tablespoons granulated sugar. Let sit 48 hours before using.

> 1   cup heavy cream
> 1   package Whip-It® or Dream Whip®
> 2   Tablespoons vanilla sugar

In a mixing bowl, combine the heavy cream, whipped topping mix and sugar. Beat at high speed until stiff (do not overbeat). Use a pastry bag with a #2B star tip to pipe whipped cream on top of the frozen cupcakes, swirling into a soft ice cream cone shape.

Chocolate Shavings

Place an 8-ounce slab of bittersweet chocolate in a warm place for 30 minutes. Using a vegetable peeler, shave the chocolate in one direction to form chocolate curls. Decorate the top of each cupcake with a few chocolate curls. Store cupcakes in the freezer; remove five minutes before serving time.

   Yield: about 36 cupcakes

Icings &
Decorations

Larry's Lemon Icing

This icing is good on almost any flavor of cake.

> 1 pound (4 loosely packed cups) confectioners sugar
> 1 cup solid shortening
> $^1/_2$ cup unsalted butter, at room temperature
> 3 Tablespoons milk
> 1 Tablespoon water
> 2 Tablespoons lemon extract
>   rind of 1 lemon, grated
>   pinch of salt
> 3-4 drops yellow food coloring
>   peel of 1 lemon, sliced for Lemon Twists*

In the bowl of an electric mixer, combine all the ingredients, except for the lemon rind. Mix at low speed until moistened, then beat for 2-4 minutes at high speed, or until icing is smooth and creamy.

Yield: enough icing for 24 cupcakes

To Ice Cupcakes: Fit a pastry bag with a #4B star tip. Fill pastry bag with icing and in a circular motion spread icing over the tops of the cupcakes, until it peaks (it should look something like an ice cream cone). Place a lemon twist on top of each cupcake.

*To Make Lemon Twists: Slice the ends off lemon. Cut the lemon in half lengthwise. Peel the rind off the lemon as you would an orange. Cut the peel into narrow strips, lengthwise, and twist. Place one twist on top of each cupcake.

Cream Cheese Icing I

This icing is delicious on either carrot or pumpkin cupcakes. Double the recipe if you want extra icing for decorating.

> 1 *8-ounce package cream cheese, softened*
> 1¹/2 *cups confectioners sugar*
> 1 *teaspoon vanilla*
> ¹/2 *cup unsalted butter, at room temperature*

In electric mixer bowl, place all ingredients and beat until thoroughly blended and smooth. Spread icing thickly over cupcakes.

Variation: Add ¹/2 cup dark raisins, ¹/2 cup light raisins, and ¹/2 cup chopped walnuts to the cream cheese frosting, mixing well to combine. (With the raisins and nuts, the frosting can't be piped but it tastes delicious!)

Yield: Icing for 24 cupcakes

Cream Cheese Icing II

This recipe is for those who don't like a very sweet icing. Double the recipe if you need more icing for decorating.

> 1 *package (8 ounces) cream cheese, at room temperature*
> 2-4 *Tablespoons whipping cream*
> 1 *Tablespoon vanilla*

In a mixing bowl, beat cream cheese until smooth. Add whipping cream until icing reaches desired spreading consistency. Beat in vanilla. Spread generously on cooled cupcakes.

Yield: icing for 12 cupcakes

Carrot Decorations for Cupcakes

You can make miniature carrots and leaves for the tops of the cupcakes. For the decorations, you will need to reserve 1½ cups of the icing. Spread the remainder over the tops of the cupcakes.

Measure out 1 cup of the reserved icing, add some orange food paste color to the frosting and mix with a spatula. To the other ½ cup, add some green food paste coloring and mix with a spatula. (This will be the basis of the carrots and leaves.)

To make carrots and leaves, you need a #12 open tip or #3 open tip, #249 leaf tip, one coupler and 2 pastry bags. (You can use disposable or parchment bags. See illustration on page 63 showing you how to make a pastry bag.)

Place the #12 tip into the first pastry bag with the orange icing. Place the coupler inside the other pastry bag with the green icing (this will allow you to change tips). At a 45° angle, hold the #12 tip and squeeze out a straight line. When your carrot is the proper length, release pressure and pull away. That will point the bottom of the carrot. If you want to do several carrots on your cupcake you may do so using a #3 tip to connect the carrots and a #249 to place the leaves on top of the carrots. **Note:** If you reserve icing for decorations, you will need to spread the frosting thinly over the tops of the cupcakes.

#249 TIP
(GREEN ICING)

#12 OR #3 TIP
(ORANGE ICING)

White Buttercream Icing

Since this icing can be piped easily, it is perfect for making decorations. Use clear vanilla, as dark vanilla will change the color of the frosting.

    1¹/3   cups solid shortening
     ¹/4   cup water or milk
           pinch salt
       1   pound confectioners sugar (4 cups loosely packed)
       1   Tablespoon clear vanilla extract

In the bowl of an electric mixer, place all of the ingredients. Beat at low speed for 2 minutes and high speed for 6 minutes, scraping the sides of the bowl before you change speeds.

Yield: 6 cups

Chocolate Glaze

For a smooth coating, this glaze should be warm when used. I like to turn cupcakes upside down and dip them right into the glaze, but they can also be frosted with a spatula.

> 1 pound confectioners sugar (4 cups loosely packed), sifted
> 1/4 cup cocoa powder, sifted
> 1/4 cup plus 2 Tablespoons water
> 1/4 cup light corn syrup
> 2 teaspoons clear vanilla extract

Whisk together the sugar and cocoa powder.

In a saucepan off the stove, beat all ingredients until smooth. If consistency is too thin, add a little more confectioners sugar. If it is too stiff, add a few drops of water at a time until the glaze is a proper consistency.

Heat over low heat just until warm. Remove from heat.

Yield: 4½ cups

Icing Glaze

Glaze should be warm when being used. If it cools too much during use, reheat as necessary. Extra glaze can be stored in the refrigerator in a covered container.

> 1   pound confectioners sugar (4 cups loosely packed), sifted
> 1/4   cup water
> 1 1/4 cups light corn syrup
> 2   teaspoons clear vanilla extract

In a saucepan, beat all the ingredients until smooth.

Heat over a low heat until just warm. Remove from heat. Cupcakes should be cooled before putting in glaze. Turn cupcake upside down, twist in icing and lift out. Allow glaze to harden before serving.

Yield: 4 cups

Flavored Glazes: You can use any of your favorite extracts for flavoring and coloring the glaze. It will change the color of the icing to a lighter shade of the particular color you use. Follow the recipe for Icing Glaze above, substituting colored extract for clear vanilla.

For light orange: add peach extract

For light green: add mint extract

For light yellow: add pineapple extract

For beige: add rum extract

For light pink: add cherry extract

Larry's Buttercream Frosting

The use of butter in this frosting makes it richer than true buttercream icing, which uses shortening only.

$^1/2$ cup unsalted butter, room temperature
1 cup solid shortening
   pinch salt
1 pound confectioners sugar (4 cups loosely packed), sifted
3 Tablespoons milk
1 teaspoon vanilla
1 Tablespoon water

In the bowl of an electric mixer, place all ingredients and beat at low speed for 2 minutes. Scrape sides of bowl and continue beating at high speed for 2 minutes or until smooth and creamy.

Yield: 4 cups

Chocolate Frosting

Chocolate lovers will appreciate the richness of this frosting.

> 1 *pound semisweet chocolate, broken into small pieces*
> 1 *cup granulated sugar*
> 1 *cup heavy cream*

Place chocolate in the top of a double boiler. Over low heat, melt chocolate. (Do not allow water to boil or chocolate will burn. Do not allow water or any moisture to mix with the chocolate.)

When chocolate has melted, add the sugar and stir until sugar is dissolved. Add cream and heat for 5 minutes. It will look like melted chocolate.

Remove from top of double boiler. Allow frosting to cool for 5 minutes. Turning cupcakes upside down, dip tops into frosting, swirling or turning the cakes as necessary to fully coat with frosting.

Yield: 5½ cups

Decorated Baby Shoes

It easy to turn a couple of cupcakes into beautifully decorated baby shoes, appropriate for a baby shower or for baby's first birthday party. Follow the directions below, and see the illustrations for how to make the cuts.

    2 *cupcakes, any flavor*
    1 *recipe White Butter Cream Icing, page 58*
       food coloring, to tint icing

Slice the tops off both cupcakes. Leave one cupcake whole. Cut the other in half, vertically.

Turn the whole one upside down, so the widest part is on the bottom. Place the half cupcake next to it, to form the shape of a baby shoe. "Glue" the two pieces of cake together using some buttercream icing.

Use the butter cream icing to ice and decorate the shoe. Pipe on icing with a #16 tip for shoe and #3 for laces and eyelets.

Make laces and eyelets a different color by adding a little food coloring or flavored extracts to the icing. Pastel colors such as pale pink, blue, yellow or green work well.

Yield: 1 decorated baby shoe

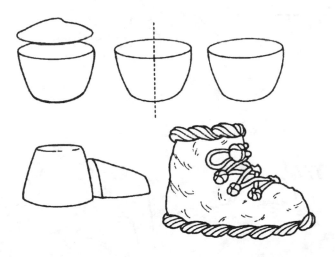

How to Make a Pastry Bag

If you don't have pastry bags, make your own disposable ones using parchment paper. Use the bags for piping icing decorations onto your cupcakes.

Supplies:
> *parchment paper*
> *scissors*
> *assorted decorating tips*

Cut baking parchment into a triangle (corners marked A, B & C).

Curl corner A around so it meets corner C. Curl corner B around so that it meets corners A and C. Fold 3 corners over back of parchment so opening is closed and tape down.

Cut ¾ inch off pointed end to accommodate the decorating tip.

See illustrations below.

Note: You can buy baking parchment at some supermarkets, at a kitchen shop or a cake decorating supply house. If you don't have parchment, substitute waxed paper or freezer paper.

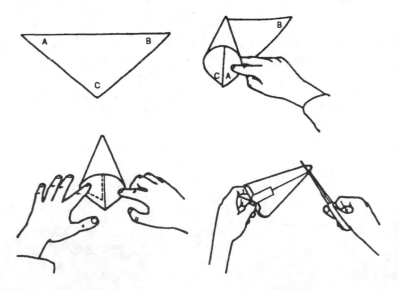